TWENTY FIFTEEN

Dedicated to those who are swamped in their silent struggle for survival and to those who have died because of our mistakes.

TWENTY FIFTEEN
Thoughts and reflections on the
First Millennium Development Goal:
To eradicate poverty and hunger

Published by Self Help Africa

Published in April 2009 by Self Help Africa
on behalf of the transition year students of
Coláiste Bhríde, Carnew, Co. Wicklow
and St. Peter's College, Dunboyne, Co. Meath.

Edited by Aideen Flood and Eleanor Lee.
Designed by Alan Davis and George Jacob.
Compiled by students Coral Barry, Sarah Brazil, Caitlín Cogavin, Megan
Callahan, Ben Cooper, Hannah Cunningham, Clara Donnelly, Cathal
Doran, Rebecca Farry, Aisling Fulcher, Caoimhe Goland, Trudie Gorman,
Anni Hayes, Zoe Horan, Orla Hughes, Dylan Hyland, Catríona Loughnane,
Sinead Murphy, Melissa Naylor, Dean O' Toole, Sarah O'Neill Murray,
Seán O'Reilly, Jennifer Patton, Sharon Rossiter, Zoe Rothwell, Seán Ryan
and Mairead Waters.

ISBN 978-0-9562452-0-5

Typeset in Whitman.
Printed in an edition of 3000 copies by Impress Printing Works, Dublin.

Printed on revive 50:50 Offset, a recycled paper containing 50% recovered
waste and 50% virgin fibre and manufactured at a mill accredited with
ISO14001 environmental management standard. The pulp used in this
product is bleached using a Totally Chlorine Free (TCF) process.

Contents

Foreword

If you can read these words you are 'wealthier' than two thirds of the people on our planet who cannot afford an education. From its conception in 2008 to its launch in May 2009 this book project took nine months and as you read through the contributions you will see that the family that nurtured this book is a caring and wonderful group of people. When 'TWENTY FIFTEEN' enters your family we know that you too will nurture and grow the thoughts shared by our contributors as if they were your own. We hope these reflections will inspire you to act against the injustice of the world we have created and help change that forever.

The inspiration for this book came from the Millennium Development Goals (MDGs) and, in particular, the First Millennium Development Goal: to end Poverty and Hunger. The eight MDGs are promises made on our behalf by our political leaders and monitored by the United Nations. But that is all they are – promises. Already in year nine of a fifteen year process, we know that many of these promises are likely to be broken – targets may not be achieved. Promises are not enough. We need to act in a way that offers a sustainable future and a better life for those two billion people who share this world with us but whose 'share' is less than €1 a day.

This action is all the more significant now given the fact that the Ireland of today is a very different one to that of nine months ago and the problems of poverty are so much closer to home. Yet, we must continue to remain hopeful that we can make a difference.

In our work with young people on a daily basis, we continue to be humbled by their passion, conviction and caring attitude towards development education. We can learn a lot from our youth and the power of partnership. As Margaret Mead, an accomplished anthropologist and author once said...

'Never doubt that a small group of thoughtful committed individuals can change the world. Indeed, it's the only thing that ever has.'

Aideen Flood
Teacher, St. Peter's College, Dunboyne

Eleanor Lee
Programme Co-ordinator, Coláiste Bhríde, Carnew

Patsy Toland
Development Education Co-ordinator, Self Help Africa

SMALL THINGS CAN HAVE
AN EFFECT ON BIG THINGS

It has been said that something as small as
the flutter of a butterfly's wing can ultimately
cause a typhoon halfway around the world.

The Butterfly Effect
Chaos Theory

Preface

In September 2008 a group of us in Transition Year in Coláiste Bhríde Carnew and St. Peter's College Dunboyne came together with the idea of creating a book about poverty. After discussions between the two groups, the idea of filling a book with the thoughts and reflections of people about the First Millennium Development Goal was embraced and so 'T W E N T Y   F I F T E E N' was born.

At first we considered poverty far too big an issue for a group of transition year students. Like many, we felt it was something for governments and humanitarians to deal with. However, we quickly realised that no matter our age, and irrespective of how much power we have, we can still improve the lives of those suffering in extreme poverty, by taking the initiative and working together. So that is what we did.

Being in two different counties, our schools faced the challenge of communication but, thanks to the wonder of Skype and other digital media, we went from being complete strangers to firm friends. It has been a wonderful journey of discovery for us all in partnership with Self Help Africa and the Combat Diseases of Poverty Consortium, NUI Maynooth.

We would like to express our heartfelt gratitude to all those who made our book happen. We thank our school communities and our families for their support and we would especially like to thank our teachers, Eleanor Lee and Aideen Flood, for their belief in us.

During the creation of this book we have come to realise that it is just by chance we were born where we are born and others aren't so lucky. Our dream for you when you read and view our book of inspirational words and images is that you will realise that hope reigns above poverty. Our dream is for global powers to work in harmony as students from St. Peter's and Coláiste Bhríde have done. Our dream is that something as small as the flutter of a butterfly's wing can ultimately cause a typhoon halfway around the world.

We thank you.

Transition Year Students
St. Peter's College Dunboyne and Coláiste Bhríde Carnew

COMPELLED TO RESPOND

In Ireland, the challenges and the humiliations of hunger and poverty resonate with us in a very particular way. They echo down through the generations from An Górta Mór – the Great Irish Famine. Like many people around the world we feel compelled to respond, to take action, to campaign. Irish people have a proud history of solidarity with those less well-off than ourselves, with those who are denied the opportunities we are given. As a nation Ireland continues to play a strong role in fighting global poverty and hunger. We do so because we have a moral obligation to respond to humanitarian needs and to be true to our values. These include respect for human rights and fundamental freedoms including the right to be free from hunger and our belief in equality and in the dignity of the individual.

In challenging times we have to re-focus our efforts and to ensure that our overseas aid is making a difference to the poorest of the poor. Despite recent budgetary adjustments, Ireland is still the sixth largest donor of overseas aid in the world in per capita terms. Irish Aid, the government's programme of overseas development assistance, focuses on poverty and hunger first, on healthcare, on fighting HIV and AIDS, on improving access to education, protecting the environment and good governance – all issues that have most impact on the poor. Our assistance is mainly targeted at sub-Saharan Africa which has the greatest concentration of poor countries in the world. We work closely with those governments who are committed to democracy and improving the lives of their citizens. It is only by working with governments that we can help to facilitate the long term change that these countries so desperately need. The fight against hunger and the first millennium development goal are the cornerstones of the Irish Aid programme. Our support, and the work of NGOs is making a huge difference to the lives of many. I saw this for myself during a recent visit to Northern Ethiopia. I was hugely impressed by Irish Aid-supported schemes that provide poor people with income and food in exchange for their work on local development projects. These projects include irrigation, tree planting and the building of roads and bridges. The small amount of income earned allows families to buy food and to send their children to school.

There are still huge challenges to be overcome before the ambition of the first millennium development goal is fully realised. However, Ireland is playing its part. Our aim is to have the stories in this book become tales of past injustice. Not the daily reality for millions of people on this planet.

Peter Power T.D.
Minister of State for Overseas Development

ANGEL

I was hurrying up the escalator of the Angel tube station in London, on my way to rehearsals in Islington and late as usual. There was a great stream of people going up, going down. In the ticket area at the top were a hundred and more people, all intently heading from the stairs to the sunlit doorways. Coming across at an angle to all these people, like a salmon fly dragged against the current, was a man on his own. He was small, thin, and grey, about my own age, with a long still face. He seemed to be too old to be a drug addict somehow. The curious thing was, he passed through the people as if he had no bodily substance at all. And certainly no one looked at him. He didn't bump into anyone, but seemed to know how to move through a crowd of souls without hindrance. He was obviously real, but at the same time seemed to exist at an angle to everyone else, just as his passage across the room was at an angle to everyone else. I looked at him with great curiosity as I passed him. He didn't meet my eye, didn't expect anyone to see him maybe. What was most likely was, he had nothing. Maybe he had family, fortune, children, but now he looked absolutely alone. His clothes were covered in a slight dust, like someone who had walked through an explosion. It struck me that this man, men like him, people like him, were often written about in Irish literature, most famously in Yeats and Beckett, the wandering tramp, the homeless person. And I wondered as I passed if this man might not know a secret that everyone should ask him about, and that would benefit anyone that asked. Seemingly mired in poverty, he seemed the most human of creature there, alone, poised, indifferent, possibly even hopeful of the day, how could I know? And permanently, persistently, perfectly, moving against the tide.

Sebastian Barry

Sebastian Barry is an award winning author
who is constantly tormented by his family and animals.

—

OUT THERE

Scandals in the magazines
Gossip to be heard
It's all money, fashion, shoes, and jeans
But have you really heard?

Out there in the developing world,
Imagine it. Try.
People are starving,
They get weak. They die.
But how are they starving?
Ask me, why?

One of the world biggest killers
Poverty kills more people than the gun.
Let me introduce you to
The reason for MDG number one.

People who are forgotten
They don't know what to do
They need help, they need support
People like me and you.

So snap out of your wishful thoughts,
Where the world's problems don't exist.
Get up, get involved, take action, resist.
Help them resist the greatest threat of them all,
Help them recover from this devastating fall.
Help them become confident,
Help them break free,
Break free from a life of poverty.

Dylan Hyland

*Dylan Hyland is a transition year student in
St. Peter's College, Dunboyne who loves music.*

I once heard a put down from an old Donegal man who had done well in the world but had never forgotten the hard times of his youth. He quoted a typical fierce remark country people used to make about the likes of himself, somebody who had risen from a very poor background to enjoy some kind of position and prosperity in the local district. 'I knew that fellow', the expression went, 'when he was running around, looking in the windows at other people's bread'.

Colourful speech, all right, but cutting too. Also a stark reminder of the reality of poverty and a reminder to us in the well-fed world there are millions looking through the windows at us, overeating and oblivious of them, indifferent as Dives was to Lazarus at the gate. Blessings therefore on the conscience-stirring work of the Young Social Innovators in Dunboyne and Carnew.

Báil o Dhia ar an obair.

Seamus Heaney

Seamus Heaney is one of the most celebrated Irish poets who won the Noble Prize for Literature in 1995.

I DON'T NEED TO BE TOLD

Sitting here in the dark
Staring at the moon
Whenever will this hunger end?
Will it be soon?

We miss breakfast and lunch
And dinner too
A nourishing meal
Is well overdue.

Before father died
He was a living sin
He used our little money
On whiskey and gin.

I shiver softly
The house is cold
Times are getting worse
I don't need to be told.

Deirdre Finn

Deirdre Finn is aged 12 and a student at Goggin's Hill National School in Cork.

ADDIS STORY

Last summer I had the privilege of spending some time in Addis Ababa, Ethiopia. As you would expect of the capital of one of the poorest countries in the world there are many people begging on the street. Every evening on my way to the local shop I used to pass four young boys. They were 12 to 14 year olds who had come to the city to try and find a better life only to end up living on the street at a busy junction. They had no possessions except for the torn clothes on their backs and they slept on the pavement sharing one blanket. They had little chance of finding proper work and even less of ever going to school or knowing the family life that we so often take for granted. Life is very tough for them but even tougher at this time as it was the rainy season. The rainy season in Addis can produce torrential rainfall. On one occasion as I passed I found them trying to eat directly off the concrete road as the rain washed their morsels away. Of course they would ask for help as I walked by but their request was always clarified with 'we will share'. Once after giving some money to the oldest boy, one of the younger ones continued to beg. He was immediately pulled back and told by the older not to ask again as I had already given. They smiled and left, only wanting what was needed and not wanting to burden. Such was their gratitude, their pride and their dignity.

Eugene Lynch

Eugene Lynch is an art teacher in Coláiste Bhríde Carnew
who enjoys travelling and everything about the outdoors.

LA SEULE SOLUTION

Dans le moyen et long terme, la réduction de la pauvreté demeure la seule solution au problème de la faim en Afrique. Quand bien même la faim est causée par des facteurs tels qu'une mauvaise santé, de mauvaises récoltes, un manque d'information sur la nutrition, des conflits, etc., presque tous ces facteurs dérivent d'un problème central: la pauvreté. Les pauvres sont moins bien portant, moins éduqués et plus vulnérables aux perturbations. Le fait que la pauvreté est le problème central dans la réduction de la faim, et en fait, à toutes les dimensions du bien-être social, est clairement documenté par la Banque Mondiale dans une série d'études sur la démographie et la santé (EDS) financée par USAID.

THE ONLY SOLUTION

In the middle and long term, the reduction of poverty remains the only solution to the problem of hunger in Africa. It is true that hunger is caused by factors such as bad health, bad harvests, a lack of information on nutrition, conflicts, etc, but almost all these factors derive from a central problem: poverty. The poor are less healthy, less educated and more vulnerable to disturbances. The fact that poverty is the central problem in the reduction of hunger, and in fact, with all dimensions of social welfare, is clearly documented by the World Bank in a series of studies on demography and health (EDS: Enquête Démographique et de Santé) financed by USAID.

Jean Claude Wedraogo

Jean Claude Wedraogo works with Self Help Africa in Burkina Faso.

Running away from problems seems to be what we are good at, isn't it? Travelling to Ethiopia made me realise that we have to stop running away. Instead we need to tackle the problems and get a proper insight into what exactly is happening in the developing world. The trip was filled with moments of both happiness and sadness. Seeing the beautiful smiles on the people's faces when I would wave at them, little things like that really brought me to tears, literally. I would like to share with you one event that I am reminded of anytime I speak about poverty.

It was early afternoon on Wednesday 19th March. Our group gathered for lunch under the beaming sunlight beside rows of tree trunks. We each received our prepared meals that were organised by our hotel. Of course, the concept of having to eat spicy food every day did not appeal to me, so I left whatever food I couldn't finish behind in the package. Others did the same. As the food was left aside in a pile, I first heard loud screams of laughter and excitement and noticed a group of around 20 children running towards us. It wasn't us they were interested in, but the food. They were aged between four and 10 years. They searched through every single plastic container, devouring any leftovers they could find. I could feel my heart in my throat as I watched one boy, no older then five years old, pick up the last container which barely had a handful of spaghetti in it. He was so cute, his chubby cheeks and adorable brown eyes. His plastic fork claimed the food that was now his. The little boy cherished his prize as if it was a Christmas gift, something that he would not receive again for a long time. As I watched him, he took little interest in me, just the scraps. I could feel my eyes burning as I tried to hold back tears. Everyone else in our group was busy in discussion, so I presumed I was the only person who was paying attention to the children. Why was this happening? I didn't want them to be treated second best to us. If I had known that these children were waiting for us to finish our meals, I would've left as much food as possible for the child. As we were moving off, a man stood in front of the boy and held out his hand. When the boy looked up at him with merciful eyes, the man snatched the container from him and threw it into the rubbish bags. The boy wasn't even finished eating. I could both see and feel his sadness. I hope this story touches your heart as it did mine. Words cannot describe what I felt.

Dervilla Reilly

Dervilla Reilly is a student in Moyne Community School, Co. Longford.

About 25,000 people die every day of hunger
or hunger-related causes, according to the
United Nations. This is one person every three
and a half seconds, and it is children
who die most often.

Hunger and World Poverty Sources:
United Nations World Food Program,
Oxfam, UNICEF 2009

The life of a freelance artist can be a fairly rackety one. In the course of my working life, there have been hard years and easier ones, and no great certainty about what would come next. The amazing thing about being poor, I have found, is that you can think of nothing else. When we say that poverty is a trap, it also traps you in your own fears. It is a spiritually debilitating state. The surprising discovery I made is that it doesn't take much money to be happy, and the sum of that basic happiness is not greatly increased by an increase in your bank account. All we need is enough - to live a life that is meaningful and free. Below that line we are in the horrors, far above it a kind of dissatisfaction sets in. 'Enough' does not seem like a lot to ask for, but we live in a world in thrall to the idea of 'too much'; dizzy with it. The place to start, if we are to work on world poverty, is with our own delight in excess; our own exuberant greed.

Anne Enright

Anne Enright is an acclaimed Irish writer
and winner of the Man Booker Prize in 2007 for her novel 'The Gathering'.

—

My first school residency was with a class of seven and eight-year old boys from an inner-city area who either had poor literacy skills, or were learning English as an additional language. The teacher was a veteran campaigner and got me in because I could draw as well as write. I had no teaching experience, so this was a very steep learning curve for me.

Never short of ambition, I decided that they would each produce a ten-page illustrated story. Some of them really struggled to write whole sentences – and if these lads could have spelled the kinds of swearwords they used when they thought their teacher wasn't listening, I would have been very happy. All the work was done orally and using pictures to start off. This was just as well, because it gave me a chance to explain that, as this work was going to be displayed in an exhibition in the children's section of a library in Dublin, we couldn't really have things like hash pipes, stabbings with syringes or flaming penises in the stories. When I told the boy we probably wouldn't be allowed display the burning penis, his response was 'What if I just had it smokin'?' It broke my heart to restrain his imagination.

But what I discovered was that these kids were bursting to tell stories. They had a wonderful way with vernacular language, loads of imagination and no inhibitions. And they had a kind of savvy that you'd never get from kids in a more protected environment. All they needed was the confidence, and we gave it to them by carrying them for the first few steps, by making everything as easy as possible, to the point where a support teacher might write out what a child told them and the child would then copy out what the teacher had written down. Or I would get them to trace the shape of a drawing and then they'd fill in the details themselves so that they could feel what it was like to create a drawing with form and proper proportions. We played and we cheated and mollycoddled them until they had each produced a ten-page illustrated story… although, granted, some of them only had two or three lines on a page.

These kids had been given a tough start in life, not just because many came from disadvantaged backgrounds, but because they had not been given much opportunity to learn one of the most fundamental lessons in life: how to try and fail and try again. We took the first few steps in helping them overcome this fear of failure, if only in the realm of storytelling. Children in these circumstances are capable of so much; they just need encouragement and a bit of guidance. But as long as they are forced to live in the kinds of unforgiving environments that poverty creates, without the necessary encouragement, they will always be reluctant to strive, to show initiative and to think long-term. And that is bad for our society as a whole, and reflects poorly on us all.

Oisín McGann

Oisín McGann is a writer and illustrator.
He lives somewhere in the Irish countryside where he won't be heard shouting at his computer.

THE POWER OF CHILDREN

'If you want to preserve knowledge
and enable it to travel through time,
entrust it to children.'

Quote from African Wisdom.

Emily Logan

Emily Logan is the first Ombudsman for Children in Ireland.

TEACH ME

You gave me a drink
and I wasn't thirsty that day,
But you taught me how to dig a well
and I haven't been thirsty since.

Prof. Ivor Brown

Prof. Ivor Brown is a writer and psychiatrist.
He is the former chief psychiatrist of the Eastern Health Board and a brilliant flute player.

—

LET THEM KNOW

Let them know, that we hear
Their tales of woe, their tales of fear
Their songs that teach, troubles far and near
Although we're here, remember we're near
It's their song, we're singing here.

YOU who are hungry
YOU who are afraid
YOU who are needy
YOU who want a change
YOU who have passion
YOU who have fire
YOU who are waiting
To be inspired

Oh let them know, that we care
Brothers and sisters, all you out there
Come sing with us, sing from everywhere
We're all united, to show we care
We know you're singing, we know you're scared
Oh let them know, that we care.

People please listen, open your eyes
We sing for a reason, we sing for what's right
People stand up, fight for your life
We're changing our ways; we're shining our light.

Transition year students and Liam Ó Maonlaí

Song composed by transition year students, St. Peter's College, Dunboyne in 2007,
with singer/song-writer Liam Ó Maonlaí.

Anyone who chooses to enter the arena of peace and justice must have a deep desire for unity, a desire that is profound and inclusive and that goes deep within us to the place where we are all one and that it is strong enough to stay steadfast and alive even under the worst of circumstances.

When our desire for peace and justice is strong and durable it flows over to peace and justice around us and we take it with us wherever we go. It becomes our practice. We are here with and for peace and justice and that is visible in everything we say and do. As we meet, as we plan, as we speak and as we march, peace and justice is at the heart of it.

Sr. Stanislaus Kennedy

Sr. Stanislaus Kennedy is a charismatic innovator in championing social issues.
She is founder of Focus Ireland and co-founder of Young Social Innovators.

A FAREWELL LETTER

Dear Free-Market Capitalist System,

Hiya. It's me. How you've been getting along? Oh dear. Kind of a tough year for you, wasn't it? You've been having a bit of a hard time in 2008, collapsing and ailing and generally being miserable, and gasping and puffing like a broken-down train, so I thought I'd drop you a line just – y'know – to offer sympathy. And – y'know - to say goodbye.

Need a hug? C'mere, ya big lunk. Let me put my arms around you. They've been saying very very nasty things about you, haven't they? Poor diddums. Come cry on my shoulder. The poor snookums dote. There, there. Oh the poor wickle capitalist bunnykins.

You're feeling unwanted. It happens to us all from time to time. Some people think the world shouldn't be organised like a slum that happens to have a casino attached. Crazy, I know! Deluded, left-wing fools. There's this childish, ludicrous, SENTIMENTAL idea that we produce more than enough in the world for everyone to be happy, that no child needs to starve, that nobody need be poor, that hunger could be eradicated all over the planet with less food than we throw away. I know, I know – bloody old hippy nonsense. What the Hell is this, the girl-guides?? Why don't they all join hands and sing 'Kum-ba-ya', right? The muesli-eating, incense-sniffing, recorder-playing eejits, with their naïve bloody ideas and their flared bloody trousers and their Bob Dylan albums and their Che Guevara posters. You know what I'd do? I'd REPOSSESS some sense into them. That'd soften their cough for them now.

You're the system that really works best. Free Market Capitalism. You're a lovely little system. You're the answer to everything! If only we could see it. I mean, okay, you chew up our pensions, devalue our houses, cause runaway inflation and rocketing fuel prices, keep half the world starving when the other half is obsessed with dieting, and the people who work hardest own the very least of everything, while the people who do no work at all own the most. But that's 'natural', isn't it? The natural order. Survival of the fittest and all that crack. I mean, yes, when I say 'survival of the fittest', I obviously don't mean it literally. Because when you break down - as you do now and again - the governments all rush to fix you. They take our money and use it to bail out the banks and the insurance companies and the oil companies and their friends. NATIONALISE THE BANKS the lefty moaners used to cry. George Bush is doing it now – the bloody commie! Because the banks don't make enough profit. Oh no. Not at all. The banks are actually CHARITABLE institutions. They're the Vincent de Paul with free cash-cards. All those times they loaned hundreds of thousands to people who couldn't afford the repayments – the banks only wanted to give people a chance. We should be GRATEFUL to them. But do you think we are? That's right. We're so selfish. Eaten bread is soon forgotten. Oh, Capitalist System. All the fantastic things you have given us over the years: wars, poverty, class divisions, inequality, the way poor people die far sooner than their rich and overfed neighbours – what kind of world would it be without you?

Some people say the model of society should be the family. From each according to their abilities. To each according to their needs. But we all know those families are very, VERY inefficient. It would be far better if mothers charged babies for giving them life, and if elderly parents paid their children for feeding them once in a while. That's the kind of world we'd all like to live in. The survival of the fittest! The natural order! Efficient, profitable, and free.

Some people think the point of life is – you know – happiness. Stuff like that. Bloody students. Swilling down the lager and chucking midgets around the disco, and they've the neck to be giving lectures to the rest of us. But who could disagree with your view, dear Capitalist System, that we're a nasty, greedy, self-serving species, venal, corrupt, brutal and violent, and that is what we are meant to be. And the POINT of our lives is to grub around like dung-beetles, amassing the biggest pile we can get. Care about each other? Yeah, right. Give the other guy a break? I'll give him a COMPOUND FECKIN FRACTURE. You are the only system that can really protect us. So I don't mind you repossessing my house, losing me my job, vanishing me my savings, starting the occasional arms race, filthying the planet – you mischievous little rascal! You do have your little ways, don't you? I don't mind that a nurse is paid far less than a man who owns a media empire, or that a teacher is paid a fraction of what an arms dealer makes. Free market, right? Way it has to be. It's all a question of motivation.

In the Communist countries they used to have these phoney 'elections' every now and again, where everyone essentially believed the same thing; it was really just moving around chess pieces. But we're lucky in the democratic world. We don't have that. Every four years, we have this completely different thing we call 'an election', where we decide which group of people, most of whom believe the same things, are going to implement you over the next while. It's not really politics – it's more a question of management. Oh we put up a lot of posters and fight phoney little wars, a bit like two gangs of overactive kids in a playground, lashing at each other with paper swords, while the classroom, and the city, and the country, and the world, are being sold to the highest bidder. It seems to work for us very well. We wouldn't want to try nasty 'regulation' or 'planning' or – ewww!! – 'working together' or anything. It just doesn't work. Not like you do.

Here's the deal you offer: The only game in town. People sell their labour. They get money. They buy food with the money. The food keeps them alive. So they can sell their labour the next day. And meanwhile the people in Africa starve, because the governments in wealthier countries break their promises. Like, what in the name of God could be fairer than that?? And yet some people say there has to be more to life. Some people say this is a bit like a burglar breaking into your house and offering to sell you back your stuff at a profit. But some people would say that, of course. Studenty bloody losers. Nuke 'em!

But I'd better sign off. You'll have things on your mind. You've a famine to cause somewhere, and that's a great thing, right? Hey you did it here in Ireland once! Worked like a treat. Because someone's always going to make money out of that too, aren't they? All those things we call 'natural disasters' or 'acts of God'. You and I know the truth. It's not God or nature at all. You don't like taking the credit. You're so modest, you really are. So take care now, Free Market Capitalist System. You did a really great job for us, all those years we had you. Missin you already.

Joseph O'Connor

Joseph O'Connor won an egg-and-spoon race at the age of seven. It still hasn't sunk in.

Two billion people live on less than €1 a day.

World Health Organisation, 2009

SHAME

Imagine a town the size of Bray being
wiped out every single day of every
week, month and year. On and on.

Twenty five thousand people die
EVERY DAY from hunger.
Not because there isn't enough food
for them, but because they are too
poor to buy or gain access to it.

Shame on all of us.

Alan Rickman

Alan Rickman is an award winning stage and screen actor born in London to Welsh and Irish parents.

How many times have we said 'I'm starving' and not understood the realities of starvation? Every day upwards of one billion people are hungry, many are starving. Achieving the Millennium Development Goal of halving the number of people suffering from hunger and malnutrition by 2015 is vital for these people. In 2007 prices of grains and rice rose dramatically, hitting the world's poorest people. Commodity prices have dropped somewhat, but their situation is still extremely serious.

In 2005, I visited Malawi in Africa, one of the world's poorest countries, to see at first hand how action at ground level with individual families can break the cycle of poverty and hunger. Malawi has seen terrible famine but, as a result of proactive policies in recent times, it is managing to grow more food locally and feed its people. My abiding memory of Malawi is the lingering smell of smoke from smouldering roadside fires, which drive out the field mice that local people catch to supplement their diet. I travelled to Malawi with Bóthar, an aid agency specialising in sending farm animals to developing countries. In the Mweramkaka Hills we watched as farmers walked to a tiny milk processing plant, carrying their milk in plastic buckets. Each farmer has one cow, but this one animal makes a huge difference to their lives, providing them with milk to drink and money from the sale of any surplus milk. A local development agency teaches the farmers how to look after their animals.

Gertrude, a mother of eight children, told me about how her cow was making such a big difference to her life and that of her children. Her plans were to use the cash from the sale of the milk to provide a better house for the family and to educate her children. She also mentioned the health benefits for the family of drinking milk. She showed me her well-tended pasture of elephant grass and her vegetable patch - a real sign of progress. Her farm adviser, Lawrence, said she was a very hard worker and I suspect she was one of his best farmers. Ironically, since the 1980s, the amount of development aid going to agriculture projects has declined from 17% to just 3% - perhaps one of the real reasons why hunger remains the scourge of the developing world. We know that a dollar invested in agriculture is four times more effective in poverty reduction than a dollar spent in any other policy initiative, so why have we ignored it? We can no longer afford to do so.

Mairead McGuinness

Mairead McGuinness was elected as a Fine Gael member of the European Parliament in 2004.

CORRUPTION IS AN ENEMY

Dear students

Thank you for your letter about your Transition Year project about world poverty and Ireland's contribution to the Millennium Development Goal of eradication of extreme poverty and hunger.

You asked me for my personal reflections on this. First, I was very proud to be part of the Irish Government that supported the Millennium Development Goals and decided to contribute 0.7% of our Gross National Product to Official Development Assistance within a specific time frame. I remember when the Taoiseach made that announcement in September 2000 at the United Nations, and I remember how proud I was of the contribution made by the Minister of State for Overseas Aid at the time, my colleague and friend, Liz O'Donnell. It is a challenging goal, but I believe in setting challenging goals in all aspects of policy – even if, at times, people criticise us for not achieving everything we want within the time frame we hoped for. Without big vision, big ambitions and big challenges, I don't think we would ever achieve great things in life or as a country. I do believe we are making good progress towards this goal. Next year, we will be donating about 0.56% of GNP to helping the less well off in the world – nearly €900 million. This puts us in the top six countries in the world by this measure.

The Irish people have a great and generous tradition of helping the poorest of the world. Even at a time when we face very difficult economic challenges ourselves, I do think it is right to continue a high level of support for the less well off. That underlines all the more that we have to work hard to ensure that these funds, Irish taxpayers' money, are well spent towards eliminating poverty. This is very important to sustain public support for our overseas aid budget. I think it is also very important that you carry out the project you have chosen to raise awareness. Ultimately, we as a country, and the Government, will sustain this level of funding if there continues to be public support for it. People need to know what is happening and what is being achieved with their money. This is a constant task and I am glad to see you are contributing to it.

One important aspect of eliminating poverty in developing countries is to promote health through fundamental public health measures like clean water, good sanitation and vaccination programmes against the most common infectious diseases.

More broadly, I believe poverty is reduced very effectively by economic opportunity and growth that all in society can participate in. This is a fundamental goal of our overall aid policy too. Open trade and investment are totally compatible with donating aid. It means empowering people to fulfil their potential; creating the conditions in which economic opportunity can be taken up; fostering trade and investment, and building a culture of enterprise and success, even in the smallest of ways. There are many aspects of this work: from opening up world trade and reducing barriers to exports from developing countries, to stimulating consumer support for their products.

Finally, I believe that one thing that is particularly important for economic development, and therefore the elimination of poverty, is to have a system of open, fair, transparent markets based on the rule of law. Corruption is an enemy of economic and social development. That is why it is important that we support high standards of governance in developing countries, no less than in our own, without any attitude of superiority.

I wish you every success with your project.
Yours sincerely,

Mary Harney, T.D.

Mary Harney, T.D. is Minister for Health and Children.
(This letter was written in Autumn 2008)

WHAT HAVE WE LEARNED?

In 1980 a major enquiry concluded that nearly a third of the Irish population (then a mere 3.2 million) was living below the poverty line, and that social inequality was greater in Ireland than any other EU country.

A generation later, at the turn of the twenty-first century, personal wealth in Ireland had reached record levels, economic growth had powered the country to the top of the international league, and a 2007 survey decided there were now 33,000 millionaires in the country. But even at the high point of the Irish boom, while absolute poverty had declined, relative poverty was increasing. According to that 2007 survey, 5% of the population owned 44% of the wealth, and within those reassuring 33,000 millionaires, small super-elite (mostly resident abroad for tax purposes) owned most of the money.

For a historian, it is hard not to look back at the early nineteenth century. Even before the devastating potato famine of the 1840s, the problem of Irish poverty preoccupied armies of statisticians, political analysts and (British) government commissions – as well as nationalist critics. With a fertile country and an intelligent, healthy population, why were the Irish still so poor? Clearly, the answers looked different from each side of the Irish Sea. But one area where Irish nationalists agreed with British economists was in blaming the huge amounts of land owned by a relatively small number of people, many of whom lived outside the island. That long-gone Ascendancy reminds me of their economic descendants nowadays, the non-resident super-elite.

What have we learned? Now the boom is over, what will happen to relative poverty? There is a New Poor as well as a New Rich in Irish society, and the spectre of unemployment has returned.

The fabled years of the Celtic Tiger brought great prosperity for many. There is a new kind of poverty in the land: the poverty of ignorance. If poverty was partly – if unevenly – conquered in the last generation, it reflected a society where education was traditionally valued. If that valuation diminishes or disappears, we lose a weapon to combat poverty in individual lives. We also lose the possibility of understanding why poverty itself persists for so long, in so many forms.

Roy F. Foster

Roy F. Foster is a historian, author and professor of Irish History at Oxford University.

HAPPY DAYS

I remember going to school 1937-1944, the boys in their bare feet, the girls wearing shoes or sandals. For our lunch we had home made brown bread and home made jam. We brought cocoa in bottles at lunch time and we heated them on the master's pot belly stove. Sticks for firing for the stove were chopped by the boys in the school yard. My mother bought a sheep's head and pluck from a small butcher who came around once a week. From the sheep's head we ate the brains and the head was boiled and well strained. The next day loads of vegetables were added and this was dinner for a couple of days. We also ate the sheep's hearts and liver. We had lots of potatoes and vegetables growing as my father was a great gardener.

My mother was a great cook and a really good dressmaker. She made all our clothes until we got too big. We ate lovely sandwiches made with parsnip well cooked and mashed with sugar and banana essence. There were no bananas during the war.

We had no cars so we walked everywhere and you were lucky to have a bike. Our family walked every Sunday to my grandparents' home and my grandmother would have a lovely apple or rhubarb tart made in a bake pan over an open fire. When she turned it out on a big dish we would get spoons and spoon out the lovely juice.

There were no bathrooms in our young days, just outdoor toilets. Bathing was on a Saturday night in a tin bath in front of a big open fire. There was no electricity, only candles, and then we got a paraffin lamp. Neighbours were great to one another, they helped in every way they could. We cut our own turf and during the summer enjoyed great days in the bog saving the turf. We would be in our bare feet with mud up through our toes. I made my first loaf of bread at seven years of age; a neighbour called and gave me sixpence for it.

Looking back they were very happy days. No one had money, we had time to visit our neighbours and chat, we entertained one another. Young people now might think we missed out on a lot but I wouldn't change my young days for anything. They were very happy times.

Betty Brown

Betty Brown is a native of the Carnew area and is an active member of the Home First Project.

'Poverty is a scourge well-known to Ireland and America. Societies that have the capability of addressing poverty, but don't accept the responsibility, will not be perceived as fair and just. Government commitment and private initiative are the tools and resources for finding and funding solutions to poverty. With government and individuals working together, the pain and waste of poverty can be reduced and perhaps, someday, eliminated.'

Thomas C. Foley

Thomas C. Foley is the former United States Ambassador to Ireland.

DAY DREAMS

More than 1.1 billion people survive on less than one dollar a day. As that thought crosses my mind I come thundering back to reality. My day dreams about the places I will visit, the shows I will see and the things I will buy in New York City this week come abruptly to an end. Instead my guilty mind is filled with the images of starving orphans that we saw in RE class. I reflect on the millions of people who will struggle for food, shelter and clean water to drink this week. For this week their main aim is to survive. Looking out the plane window at the world below me I am horrified by the unfairness and inequality in our world. How many people will starve to death in the seven hours it takes me to travel to the USA? I think about my designer purse bulging with dollars. In one week I will spend hundreds of dollars on unnecessary luxuries. This would be enough money to feed many, buy urgently needed medical supplies, or install fresh water pumps in developing world countries. I could help people who desperately need to be saved. I feel selfish when I imagine all the young people my age who are forced to work long hours, enduring terrible conditions and only earning less than one dollar a day. Their life is so shocking, so disturbing, so tragic and most of all so unlike my own life that I can't even imagine myself in their shoes. When the air hostesses come around collecting money for charity, I donate what I can. Everyone must play their part to eradicate poverty and make the world a better place for everyone.

Sarah Kelliher

Sarah Kelliher is a student at St. Wolstan's Community School, Celbridge, Co. Kildare.

I AM THE BOY

I am the boy on O'Connell Bridge
Hand outstretched in the rain
Freckled, long and grimy brown
Scowling through the shame.

I am the traveller boy you see
Standing by the motorway
Living in a trailer house
To the sound of trucks and cars all day.

I am the boy from the Island Field
Hunched up shoulders like my mates
When Santa came to me last year
He left a knife and a little hate.

I am the boy on Patrick Street
In a cardboard box in the cold night air
No bed, no heat, no gentle Ma
To tuck me in, or soothe my fear.

I am the boy in your own town
Worthless, troubled, dull, in need
No home, no care, no love, no school
And you walk by and pay no heed.

Martin Phillips

*Martin Phillips is Education Officer for Wicklow VEC
and is interested in hill-walking and photography.*

One of the largest concentrations of poverty in the world exists in sub-Saharan Africa. In my part of the world, not being poor is the exception to the rule. When I came to Ireland to work for three months with the Combat Diseases of Poverty Consortium, NUI Maynooth, I quickly realised the opposite is the case in Ireland. However, before leaving Ireland in November 2008 to return to my beautiful Uganda, I realised that there are great things happening in schools in Ireland. On my visits to schools on the CPDC Outreach Programme, I found that students and their teachers were actively engaging with issues in the developing world. After my visit to Coláiste Bhríde, Carnew, I came away with a smile on my face as I realised that these students really will make their community, Ireland and sub-Saharan Africa a more equal place for us all, through their active global citizenship.

Keep up the good work and see you in Uganda some day.

Dr. Kalule John Bosco

Dr. Kalule John Bosco is currently pursuing a Masters of Medicine in Microbiology at Makerere University, Kampala, Uganda.

Norway, Sweden, Denmark, Luxembourg and
The Netherlands have already reached the
0.7% MDG goal.

OECD 2008

'No Eyes, No Voice' by Jennifer Hart

Jennifer Hart is an established artist who began her painting career by painting celtic manuscripts on glass which brought colour and vibrancy to her work which she transferred onto canvas.

Drought   Jakub Galka   6th cl

Cargsfort N.S.

'Woman planting' by Liz Hayes

Liz Hayes is an accomplished artist and mother
who tries to infuse everything in her life with creativity.

'The new rains will come down soon' by Fiona Fahey

Fiona Fahey is a 6th year student in St. Peter's College, Dunboyne.

'She is dying' by Mica Warren

Mica Warren is a fifth year student in Coláiste Bhríde, Carnew.

'Together' by Maria Smith

Maria Smith is a sixth year student at St. Peter's College, Dunboyne.

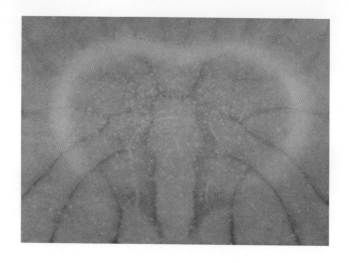

'Floating World 18' by Tim Goulding

Tim Goulding is an artist and musician.
He has lived and worked in Allihies, on the Beara Penninsula in West Cork since 1969.

'Just Another Number' by Sinéad Finlay

Sinead Finlay teaches Geography and Maths in Coláiste Bhríde Carnew and has a keen interest in amateur dramatics.

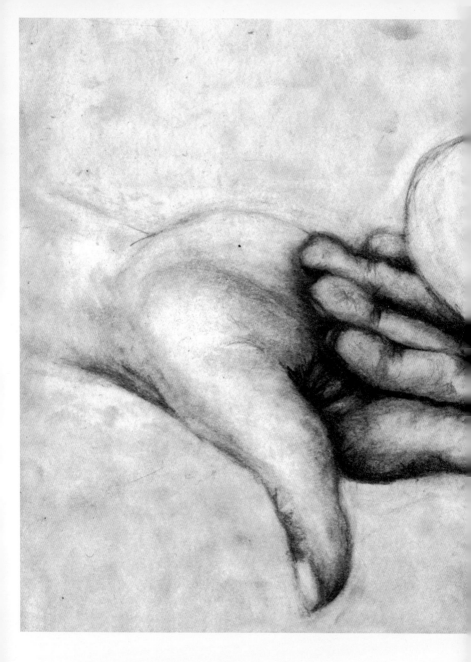

'Only through compassion and love for our fellow human beings
can we finally stop poverty' by Aidan Knowles

*Aidan Knowles is a sixth year student in St. Peter's College, Dunboyne
who has a passion for the arts.*

Aiden K.
8/9/05

'Destitute' by Chloe Phipps

*Chloe Phipps is a fifth year student in St. Peter's College, Dunboyne,
whose heart is set on going to the National College of Art and Design.*

'A Helping Hand' by Sean O'Reilly

Sean O'Reilly is a transition year student in St. Peter's College, Dunboyne.
As a result of being awful at every type of sport, he has been drawing all his life.

'Butterfly Effect' by Hannah Cunningham

*Hannah Cunningham is a transition year student in Coláiste Bhríde Carnew
who is a talented musician and artist.*

SAD LONELY EYES

The lonely old wizened man
Sat in the cold night air
Watching life go by.
Cars hooting, lorries flying and
Buses screeching,
The glimpse of light in every home,
The chimneys puffing smoke
Grey and misty.
Oh! To be warm and secure.
The rustle of cardboard
No blankets, no tea
Two sad lonely eyes
Gaze out at the world.
The old man decides to sleep
And snuggles up tightly on his bed
Slowly, slowly he falls asleep
Dead as a door mouse
And to the cold world around him.

Conor Fanning

Conor Fanning is a first year student in Coláiste Bhríde and has a keen interest in rugby.

A TELLING EXAMPLE

The poor give us so much more than we give them.
They're such strong people, living day to day with no food,
and they never curse, never complain.
We don't have to give them pity or sympathy.
We have so much to learn from them.

Mother Teresa.

I have been privileged to spend time over the past few years in the developing world, both in Mother Teresa's Calcutta and in several African countries, and I have been hugely impressed by the ability of people to triumph over extreme poverty: poverty that we on this side of the world would be incapable of enduring.

A simple but telling example of this resilience happened on a visit to a mud hut in rural Ethiopia. The family had retrieved from our group of visitors an empty plastic litre bottle of water. By cutting it up, they managed to get five household items which they would not, otherwise, have been able to afford. The bottle cap was used to give sips of water to the baby, the neck became a very useful funnel, the middle section was cut into two cylinders which were used to protect saplings from goats and the base of the bottle was used as a cup. Apart from these five items there was nothing in the hut apart from a few mats for sleeping and a very old blackened pot for cooking. The children wore rags and there were flies hovering around them. The thought that struck me was that these people deserve our help and that when they get something, they make the very most of it.

It's an accident of birth that we are living in an affluent and highly developed part of the world and that others are living in awful squalor and poverty. I believe we, as individuals, communities and governments, have a moral responsibility to look to the needs of those who are less well off. They need our help, they deserve our help and they appreciate and make the most of any help they get.

Mary Kennedy

Mary Kennedy is one of the most recognised television personalities and is currently a presenter on Nationwide and has been the MC at the YSI Showcase for the past three years, including this year 2009.

One of the saddest things I have ever seen was a man cycling out of a camp in Soroti in Northern Uganda with a tiny coffin on the back of the bike carrying the body of his baby. He was taking their baby home, to what was left of home, to be buried. They are the victims of the torture imposed on the people of Northern Uganda by the Lord's Resistance Army (LRA). The LRA under the leadership of Joseph Koni are infamous for their 'child soldiers' policy. They burn families from their homes, kidnap their children and murder or torture the remaining villagers. The children they kidnap are brutally trained to become 'child soldiers' who are then forced to become part of the LRA and return to torture their own people. For those who do not conform, the fate is either death or to be sent back to their village minus an arm, leg, ear or nose. This is to warn others of what could be their fate. Girls as young as 12 years of age are abducted and become sex slaves for the LRA.

In 2003, when I visited Soroti with Self Help Africa, those who escaped from the villages were set up in temporary camps in school yards, fields or anywhere they felt safe. Whole families queued with great dignity for food rations supplied by various charities. There were no riots, no complaints, just a queue of helpless people grateful for what little they could get. I spoke with women who had given birth in the camp with no medical assistance and just a concrete school yard as their bed.

We cannot ignore the plight of these people. It is our duty to help. We can make a difference.

Eleanor Shanley

Eleanor Shanley is a singer from Co. Leitrim renowned for her unique interpretation of Irish music.

In sub-Saharan Africa, the proportion of people living in extreme poverty fell from 46.8% in 1990 to 41.1% in 2004. Most of this progress was achieved since 2000. The number of people living on less than $1 a day is also beginning to level off, despite rapid population growth. Nevertheless, the region is not on track to reach the goal of reducing poverty by half by 2015 – the absolute number of poor is still around 300 million.

Irish Aid
Millennium Development Goal One

Millennium Development Goal (MDG) One – The eradication of extreme poverty and hunger is inextricably part of the other seven goals and is the one by which the success or failure of the millennium project can and will be measured. In Ireland we, as individuals, cannot fully comprehend extreme poverty and hunger, although our nation and people have a close connection through our relatively recent history. When we look back to the great famine in Ireland of 1845 to 1850 we are reminded of the great injustice that lead to the deaths of over one million of our people and the emigration of a further million and regard the rich and influential of the time in a poor light. But how will future generations look back at ours? Will they see us as the wealthy and uncaring who had so much but did little or nothing to prevent millions dying each year because of an accident of where they were born?

The eradication of extreme poverty and hunger is one of the greatest challenges facing humanity. It's easy to place the blame on greedy despots as the source of the problems of developing countries, but that's just a symptom of greater underlying problems. We need to work together (MDG Eight) to empower the poor, both men and women (MDG Three) so that they have a voice and the opportunities to determine their own destiny. Education is essential to achieve this (MDG Two) as it was in our own economic development. But health is central (MDGs Four, Five and Six). There is a vicious cycle of disease and poverty for the extremely poor and malnourished.

To eradicate extreme poverty and hunger will require redistribution of resources since our society is currently plundering the earth's resources at a pace that is outstripping its capacity to regenerate. If we do not then our planet will not sustain the current and growing population. In reality, MDG One is fundamental to addressing the major challenges that face the human race, such as global warming, environmental degradation and human conflict. Ireland may be a small nation but, because of our history and recently acquired wealth, we have an important lead role to play in ensuring that this goal is not only achieved, but is sustained for future generations.

Dr. Noel B. Murphy

Dr. Noel Murphy is a lecturer at the Institute of Immunology, and the co-chair of the Combat Diseases of Poverty Consortium, National University of Ireland, Maynooth.

THE BEST WAY TO FIND YOURSELF

Mahatma Gandhi was a very wise and peaceful person. His belief was that 'poverty is the worst form of violence' in the world and that greed is a root cause of poverty. He was also a great believer in the humanity of mankind and that the resolution of poverty in the world is within us. His advice on living more humanely is I think contained in this statement made by him:

'the best way to find yourself is to lose yourself in the service of others.'

Rachel Collier

Rachel Collier is CEO and co-founder of Young Social Innovators.

Hope reigns above hardship. This was my first realisation of Kenya. I was aghast at the absolute poverty. Like most, I had previously read and viewed images, but nothing would prepare me for what I would see with my own eyes. Bare feet, coughs, runny noses, TB, AIDS. Images burned forever on my memory. The Gospel Choirs were wonderful. A natural aptitude and ability to communicate through song. The potential to reach millions. An untapped resource. An ability to make do with nothing never ceased to amaze me. Being dealt an unfair hand, they survive against all odds, never going down without a fight. Incredible smiles on beautifully sculpted faces. I wondered what they had to smile about. Over time, realisation dawned. Kenyans have an enviable faith. They have pride and dignity and an amazing sense of community. Are these not riches in themselves? We could learn a lot from our hosts. We have everything, yet, we have nothing. The deprivation, lack of facilities, amenities and infrastructure appalled me. The condition of the schools left me at a loss. But I am looking at this with Western eyes. The use of every single square inch of land was incredible. The work ethic, the attention to detail, the energy: amazing. The gender inequalities shocked me to the core. Are these not an absolute violation of human rights?

I see how education is their lifeline.
I see that Self Help is their saviour.
I see the strength of women.
I see the pride and dignity and the bright eyes.

Kenyans have hope and faith. Kenyans have everything.

Eleanor Lee

Eleanor Lee is Programme Co-ordinator in Coláiste Bhríde.
She believes that young people should never stop trying to make a difference.

I am not a political person in any nationalistic sense but I am political when it comes to Human Rights and the environment. We measure a society, in part, by how it looks after its most vulnerable members, which means those on the margins both in terms of age and economic standing. Therefore we must look at ourselves and wonder how we treat children, the elderly, the ill and the poor. I would like to think that I will be of a generation who passes on the planet in no worse a state than it was found at the beginning of our tenure – already with the phrase 'no worse a state' I am expecting that it will be no better and that's pessimistic in itself. However, it needn't be so when it comes to poverty.

I am a patron of World Vision Ireland, an aid organisation to the Third World so I have seen aid at work there. I am a citizen of Ireland so I only need eyes to see poverty at home and how we are handling it. It can often be insidious – not only the most raggedly dressed are the poor; there is a whole new section of society falling into the trap while seeming to be getting along fine. Social issues like the emergence of the New Poor and the further descent of the already very poor are urgent topics and concerns. As in every other country in the world, education plays a huge role in eradicating poverty and exploitation. It needs to be as closely shepherded as poverty itself.

I have travelled to Africa with World Vision to see the aid we send there at work. And it does work, when well placed and sustained. Recently, I had the honour of visiting the Gakungu region of Kenya where the organisation is phasing out aid as the community is now self sufficient and ready to go ahead alone.

At the turn of the century, the governments of the developed world made a promise to give, by 2015, 0.7% of their gross national income per annum in overseas aid. So, how are we Irish doing? Not badly at all, as it happens. The Irish government made the pledge to be on target by 2012, earlier than other countries. We are 5th in the 'League Table' behind the Scandanavians, but larger countries like Germany and the UK are well behind on their promise.

Before we get all pleased, though, let's take a kicker into consideration: although we are pretty much on-target, the country is also in recession so 0.7% now is much less than expected because we just don't have the gross national income that we did even a couple of years ago. So, less aid is available.

There's a lot of talk about tightening our belts in these parlous times but aid to those poorest both at home as well as abroad is not something that we should, or can, give up on. In fact, it is imperative that we do not - we have a duty to look after those less fortunate, simple as that. It doesn't take much on our part to make a meaningful difference. Poverty is a political issue and I'm glad that it is. We must keep it on every agenda to ensure dignity now and in the future for all of mankind: it's the very least we should do.

Pauline McLynn

Pauline McLynn is an actress, comedienne and author,
best known for her portrayal as 'Mrs. Doyle' in the series Father Ted.
(This submission was written in Autumn 2008)

THE POOR

Every hour more than 1,000 people die worldwide because of hunger and poverty. Each day one in seven of all the people in the world goes to bed hungry. Every five seconds a child from a poor family dies because of hunger. Poor mothers are more likely to die in childbirth. Children of poor families are more likely to be malnourished. Poor children receive little education and some may receive none at all. The poor are likely to be badly affected by the recent downturn in the global economy, while rising food prices are expected to push a further 100 million people into extreme poverty.

Michael Kelly

Michael Kelly is a retired Professor of the University Of Zambia (UNZA).
He has been at the forefront of research on the interconnection between education and HIV and AIDS.

More than a quarter of children under age five
in developing countries are malnourished.

United Nations 2009

WE COULD HELP

As some kids watch TV all day,
And other kids go out to play,
There are children in our world today,
Who have to walk three miles per day.

Hungry and thirsty they sit alone,
Just praying and wishing they had a home,
Growing up is a very tough time,
But theirs is worse than yours and mine.

They struggle to face the problems that come,
But there are things that must be done,
And if everyone just gave something small,
Maybe we could help them all.

Poverty is everywhere,
But still not everyone seems to care,
In countries, cities, streets and towns,
Poverty is all around.

Rebecca Stephenson and Maria Kennedy

Rebecca Stephenson and Maria Kennedy are first year students in St. Peter's College Dunboyne.

THE PROMISED LAND

On Gross-Ile, an island on the St. Lawrence River and 20 miles south of Quebec, an inscription on a monument reads:

> 'In this secluded spot lie the mortal remains of 5,294 persons who, fleeing from pestilence and famine in Ireland, found in America, not a home but a grave.'

The people who died would have left their humble homes in Ireland and walked many miles to a town they had never seen before. Dying of hunger, they would have spent six weeks at least on an overcrowded sailing vessel, having never seen the sea in their lives. They succumbed to cholera at the very gateway to their promised land.

The Irish Famine, 1847.

Kevin J. Lee

Kevin J. Lee is an artist, wood sculptor, and founder of Carnew Historical Society.

ON THE SIDE OF FREEDOM

John 12:8

When Jesus said:

'The poor are always with you'

perhaps he meant it in more ways than one.
Maybe he meant the poor are always on the side of freedom.
Maybe his words were meant as a reminder to his followers,
to all of us, that the poor are always with us, if we are on their side.

John McKenna

John McKenna is a writer who has won the Irish Times Literary Award,
the Jacobs Radio Award and the Hennessy Literary Award.

The people of Ireland have a duty to engage, both socially and culturally, with the plight of the modern world. In our affluent society, we can too often turn our focus inward. Our interaction with the greater world, even if it is only through our laissez-faire attitude to a war half the world away, has an impact. During the Ulster Bank Dublin Theatre Festival in 2008, plays like *Black Watch* sought to make the war in Iraq a cultural reality for us all. In December 2008, in a series of talks and rehearsed readings called *Bearing Witness*, the Abbey Theatre attempted to show that drama can and should provide another forum for debate.

Ireland has so far failed to achieve the First Millennium Development Goal. We must strive to point Ireland's inward gaze outwards, away from the issue of recession and towards the dispossessed families of the developing world.

Fiach Mac Conghail

Fiach Mac Conghail has been the Artistic Director of The Abbey Theatre since 2005.

WISDOM

Gathering together our personal stories, and naming and claiming our past, are critical for all of us because knowing where we have come from helps us to know where we are going. This applies not just to individuals but also to families, to communities and to organisations. It is also critical for cultures and nations to recall their history, their suffering, poverty, famines and what it was that brought them through. Especially in times of oppression and hardship, it is often a country's poets and writers who tell the stories, bear witness and hoard the memories of the people for the future. Remembering is not about wallowing in the past, it is about enabling us to live more fully in the present and leading us into the future. Do what you love and people will love what you do.

Dorcas Rothwell

Dorcas Rothwell is Chairperson of the Parents Association, Coláiste Bhríde Carnew.
Working with others and giving to others is important to Dorcas.

The greatest proportions of children going hungry continue to be found in Southern Asia and sub-Saharan Africa. Poor progress in these regions means that it is unlikely that the global target for hunger will be met. If current trends continue, the world will miss the 2015 target by 30 million children.

Irish Aid
Millennium Development Goal One

Even in this House there is not the passionate concern. We have not woken up yet to the complete scale of the matter. The report points out that governments consistently give grandiose commitments in front of the television cameras and then fail to live up to them. The population of this small planet has doubled since I did my leaving certificate. Some 860 million people are at the most critical level of poverty. People said 'never again' after the Famine, but the events about which we say 'never again' tend to happen repeatedly. We are refusing to learn lessons. The United Nations Millennium Development Goals now comprise something of a catalogue of shame. Even though our aims in this regard are quite modest, we have not achieved them.

Senator David Norris

David Norris is a member of Seanad Eireann who has been involved in many human rights issues from gay rights to Guantanamo.
(The above extract has been taken from 'Statements on the Hunger Task Force Report', October 2008)

EMPATHY THROUGH HISTORY

Poverty – Everyone will think
When they see these words, and say
'Ah sher, gawd love them' every time.

Horror can run though our minds and out again
Faster. Faster than what it takes.
The time it takes to really contemplate.

Rotting bread, worms and grubs,
Does anyone remember the Indian meal?
Sent to us from a pitying country.
Is pity really enough? Remember –
People 'gawd loved' us once, too.

Aisling Fulcher

Aisling Fulcher is a transition year student in St. Peter's College, Dunboyne who enjoys writing poetry.

SUNLESS LANES

Through our sunless lanes seeps poverty,
Through our darkened streets creeps greed,
They'll join and work together,
To kill those most in need.

Sin will arrive with a face,
That's truly ugly and grim,
Ready to rule the world,
Where tears will replace grins.

Amelia Hennessy

Amelia Hennessy is a transition year student in Coláiste Bhríde Carnew who enjoys dancing and spending time with friends.

Wherever one lives, the effects of poverty are never too far away. Washington, DC is no exception. Even within sight of the grandiose Capitol building, houses in disrepair and the homeless sleeping in parks are regular sights – extreme poverty and extreme wealth share not only the same country, but also the same neighbourhoods, the same streets.

This coexistence of poverty and wealth seems common in cities around the world. But living in Washington, where so many organizations from around the world have set up their offices, one is reminded that these phenomena do not simply coexist, but are deeply intertwined at a global level. Rich countries depend upon poorer countries and vice versa.

While recent events in the financial markets have led some to wonder if countries should focus on fixing their own economies before helping the poor and hungry outside their borders, it would be disastrous to focus solely on this one small piece of the poverty puzzle. Because of this, I am very happy to see that schools like St. Peter's, Dunboyne and Coláiste Bhríde in Carnew are mobilizing to work towards the same goal as the European Commission in encouraging Member States to fulfill their foreign aid obligations.

Even in these difficult times, it is more important than ever before for all EU Member States, including Ireland, to work towards reaching the Millennium Development Goals because poor countries will feel the recession even more than richer countries will. The health and vibrancy of one person is dependent upon the well-being of others in their community, and our community is increasingly a global one.

Ambassador John Bruton

John Bruton served as the ninth Taoiseach of Ireland
and is currently Head of the Delegation of the European Commission in Washington DC.

The sound of children singing stopped me in my tracks. What an unlikely place for enchantment: beaten earth, tumbled down shacks, a fruitless banana tree. I followed the sound, and found a school. Once perhaps it had been a colonial gate-lodge, now it was a bullet-pocked shell. The singing stopped and a tall Angolan appeared in the doorway. 'Would you like to come in?' he asked.

Some months previously I had happened to see a television programme describing a visit that Princess Diana was making to Angola, in West Africa. She wanted to reveal to the world the evils of landmines, small 'bombs' that soldiers bury a few inches below the soil to explode under the feet of their enemies. When the fighting is over, however, they often leave the landmines in the ground, where civilians, frequently children, step on them. The camera panned away from Diana, to show four children, all on crutches, and all with only one leg. Incensed at what I was seeing, I decided then and there that I must write a book about these evils. No sooner had I begun to write, however, than I realised that I would have to go to Angola to see the problem for myself. Now my trip was nearly over. I had visited a hospital, and had met landmine victims. I had been shown how mines could be found and cleared. I had met a girl called Yola, who would surely become my heroine. I had seen where a hungry boy had set a bird-trap, crouched barely foot from where a live mine had lain hidden, and today I had been shown where a mine had been placed cunningly at the foot of a cinnamon tree.

Now the man was holding out his hand. 'Welcome to my School,' he said. The school was tiny; the four rooms would have fitted into a single Irish classroom, and each was packed with children. I wondered why they were staring up at me, then I realised it was because they were all sitting on the ground on stones. 'We have no money to buy furniture,' explained my host; 'but where would we put it?' He laughed. 'But we do have a blackboard that we carry from class to class.' I smiled at the children. 'Where do they come from?' I asked. 'Oh,' he said, 'they come from farms all around here, but they can't go home because of landmines. You see, you only have to find one landmine on your farm, and you daren't go back. Where there is one there will probably be others.' The children looked expectant. I felt helpless without a common language. 'May I take a photograph of the class?' I asked. A few words in Portuguese, and there was a ripple of movement. I saw then that they all had a single work-book, and wanted to be photographed holding it. Their faces had a glow now, as if their books had already done their magic, enabling them, to read, to write, to do simple sums... in short to find a way out of their present minefield. They weren't asking for much. As I walked away their singing started again.

Aubrey Flegg

Aubrey Flegg is an Irish author who won the Bisto Children's Book of the Year in 2004.

OUR WORLD AND THEIR WORLD

The world we live in is like a see-saw that is constantly tilting in our favour, the high level being developed countries like Ireland and America and the lowest being countries stricken with poverty. However, on a see-saw surely you wouldn't leave your friend at the bottom and continue living the high life yourself? You wouldn't simply ignore their cries and pleas to help them get to your level, would you? Would you focus on enjoying yourself high up on the see-saw and turn a blind eye to whoever is unfortunate enough to be at the bottom? We'd all like to say we'd act appropriately but sadly, sometimes we don't. I traveled to Ethiopia last Easter and I saw things that shocked me into a completely different frame of mind. Ethiopia is a country that has been struck by famine on numerous occasions. Just when the people are recovering, they are plunged into starvation once more. Malnourishment is a major issue, especially among children and there are many things there that simply aren't right.

During my ten days in Ethiopia, I saw a lot of poverty but especially in the city of Addis Ababa, which has a population of over three million. The housing in the city is nothing more than slums made of old sheets of metal and dirt. The crime rate is catastrophic as there's no security of any kind. People are covering the streets and mothers sit outside their homes with their babies among the chaos. Children are everywhere, most of them street children who will be sold into slavery or even - I shivered – the sex trade and human trafficking. Their parents are long gone - who knows where? - and they're completely and utterly alone in this dangerous city. These children are wearing rags over their almost skeletal bodies and unhealthy, bloated bellies: the result of malnutrition. The young girls have learned from an early age that they are not the dominant sex. They were clearly awestruck to see that we are all equal in our country and that we can fulfill second and even third level education if we wish. Our gender is not an issue. Girls as young as twelve and thirteen are forced to be mothers to their younger siblings as they live on the streets. Mere toddlers race through the city looking for food and shelter: the basic human needs and rights. This is the world we live in, that is the world they live in. The see-saw is still very much tilting in our favor. Will it ever be even?

Sarah Carthy

Sarah Carthy is a student in Moyne Community School, Co. Longford.

FOOD FOR THOUGHT

Everyday
I think without eating.
When night falls
I wonder,
Why do crops fail?
Where is my home?
What is hope?

Everyday
I eat without thinking.
When night falls
I wonder,
Why bother with homework?
Where's the remote?
What's for dinner?

Liz McManus, T.D.

Liz McManus is the Labour Party T.D. for Wicklow and is a published author.

YOURS AND MINE

People travel to Africa
To see elephants.
Everyday, there is
An elephant in my room.
The elephant is poverty.
It's your elephant and mine.
Time to remove it.

Joseph Clowry

*Joseph Clowry is Education Officer with the Combat Diseases of Poverty Consortium,
National University of Ireland, Maynooth.*

Standing by the 4x4 parked on a lonely dirt road overlooking the African rolling hills of KwaZulu Natal I got my first real taste of Africa. They say that once you have the sand of Africa on your shoes it never really leaves you. As I sit here today, looking out of my kitchen window, I can still feel the sun on my face and recapture the sense of space and the feeling of freedom. It was a rare moment of feeling content and complete.

Thirty minutes later I was walking through the corridors of a hospital. Nothing could have prepared me for the contrast. It was as if there had been some kind of disaster, such a massive influx of people into the hospital that it couldn't cope with the volume of patients that had suddenly arrived.

It was difficult to navigate through the corridors due to the amount of people lying on surgical trolleys, propped up in chairs or just lying on the concrete. The wards themselves were so full that patients were sleeping on the floors between the beds or at the end of them. One lady leaned to prop herself up off the floor.

The people in the beds were living skeletons. It was impossible to tell if they were alive or dead. This wasn't a hospital anymore, it was a place for people with HIV/AIDS to come and die. I stopped by one bed. A sheet covered a frail woman. I knew the sheet was just waiting to be pulled that last foot over her head. I felt so many emotions collide. Confusion, sadness, anger. But above all I felt guilt. Guilty to be intruding into the last moments of this lady's life. There was no one with her. I'm not a religious person but I quietly asked for God to look after her. As I sit here today, I can feel the tears well up again. HIV in the western world is 'just a disease'. In rural communities in Africa death from HIV/AIDS is often brutal and undignified.

Two years ago I met a 10-year-old boy. He was a lovely kid, one that everyone warmed to. He'd lost his parents to HIV/AIDS and he himself was HIV positive. A year ago, I saw him again; he was still the cheeky boy I remembered. I traded a Swiss army knife with him – I remembered all the fun I'd had with one when I was his age. A month ago I was back in Africa. Oopmie had died from AIDS two weeks before I got there.

Duncan Goose

Duncan Goose quit his job in business in London to travel the world on a shoe-string. In 2004 he established the not for profit organisation Global Ethics.

LIFFEY BRIDGE

A drunken beggar falls asleep,
wine seeping from wind-broken lips.
Sealed into his swollen being,
he sleeps on a cold bridge and dies.
The wonder of lights on water,
its high Sierras! A closed box
of closed thoughts: the proud dead cock
that never crowed.

Philip Casey

Philip Casey is a writer and member of Aosdána, the organisation established by the Arts Council of Ireland to honour those artists whose work has made an outstanding contribution to the arts.

Two Americans sat at an enamel table talking loudly above the chimes and flight announcements. Both were bald and overweight. The smaller was the older by far, could have been the big one's father. His head was freckled with age spots. He took out his wallet and produced English notes of different denominations. He had a big cigar stub in the right side of his mouth. At no time did he remove it - not even to talk.

Behind them a trolley was piled high with aluminium cases, overcoats and hats. The younger one got up and went to the trolley and produced a paper cup with LIGHTNING written on it. He sat again and opened a small green tin. With a finger he hooked something black out of it and popped it in his mouth. After a while he lifted the paper cup and sipped from it.

He produced his wallet again. Some money changed hands. The old man looked closely at the notes' denominations, held them up to the light. The other sipped again - yet it wasn't like real sipping. He raised the cup but did not tilt it. It was as if he was about to drink then at the last second he would change his mind.

He was chewing tobacco and spitting like a rabbit - if such a thing can be imagined - lifting his top lip and squirting downwards into the cup. When their flight was announced the small man stood. The big one eased his head into a white Stetson, then hooked a finger inside his mouth and dropped something black into the cup. He had a final spit and set the cup back on the table. They gathered themselves and the small one led off with a gold topped cane. He didn't lean on it, but twirled it like a band leader. The big one pushed the trolley after him - round-shouldered, shambling, looking out from under the brim of his Stetson.

An Asian cleaning woman in a turquoise overall, wiping and tidying, gradually worked her way towards the mess on the table the Americans had just vacated.

Bernard McLaverty

Bernard McLaverty is a Belfast born author
who writes as a way of trying to make sense of a difficult world.

ACT

'It is not enough to be compassionate; you must act'

The Dalai Lama, Tenzin Cyatso (1992)

Fiona Hartley
Fiona Hartley is CEO of Co. Wicklow Vocational Education Committee.

LEARN

To learn is to change the world.

Eamonn Gaffney
Eamonn Gaffney is the principal of St. Peter's College, Dunboyne.

PARTNERSHIP

There are many reasons to value education, the most important being that it is a way out of poverty. Let us work together in partnership.

Linda Dunne
Linda Dunne is the principal of Coláiste Bhríde, Carnew.

HOPE

Our young people offer us the greatest hope to make the world a better place.

Peter Kierans
Peter Kierans is CEO of Co. Meath Vocational Education Committee.

One year, it was decided to cancel Christmas altogether. The government rushed through emergency legislation which placed an embargo on all seasonal festivities. No gifts, no cards, no last minute panic in the shops. The cost of wrapping paper alone, it was argued, would abolish world poverty overnight. People were asked to place the money they would have spent on Christmas gifts into a fund which then went towards a development project in Guatemala. An NGO agency on the ground was chosen to make sure that the money went directly to the people who needed it most. It became known as the Guatemalan Chicken Project. An agricultural credit union was set up, whereby people in remote villages in the hills could borrow the means to buy chickens and once they sold the chickens for profit, they could pay back the loan. Ongoing reports were published on how the Christmas money was being spent to generate income in one of the poorest regions of the world.

Up to then, the government had been relying on the old economic principles that having Christmas was actually good for the poor. It was called the 'trickle down' effect. The more people consumed, the more they were spreading their wealth around and the more the people in those poorer places were likely to prosper as well. That was the theory, at least. They were told that spending was a patriotic act. Economic growth was good for everyone, all round, experts were often heard repeating. Generosity began at home and then flowed out to the poor by default. Eradicating hunger and poverty was based on this well-known, 'trickle down', model of natural distribution. All they had to do is become wealthier and consume more. The open market would ultimately ensure that their spending would leak through the floorboards down to the people underneath. The more Christmases the better. The more generous people were to themselves, in other words, the more the people below them would also feel the water table of wealth rising. But then came the financial crisis and everybody realised the hard facts that the old 'trickle down' principles were really just keeping people in the same poverty forever. The trickle was never enough. It was like running to stand still. So the government was forced to act swiftly and abolish Christmas altogether. At least, it was placed on hold until extreme poverty was dealt with. Once that was achieved, the government pledged, Christmas could be reinstated in due course.

Hugo Hamilton

Hugo Hamilton is the award winning author of
'The Speckled People' and his greatest wish would be to stare a grizzly bear in the eye.

THE STORY OF AYELECH

Ayelech Mama has been living with HIV/AIDS for five years. A mother of five from Lode Hitosa Woreda (district) in Ethiopia, she speaks of the 'dark days' after a blood test diagnosed that she had the virus, an event that was followed not long afterwards by the death of her own husband. 'The level of stigma in my village was so deep, it existed in our everyday life. It also reinforced fears in our family members, neighbours and outsiders. Life was so hard', she recalls.

The burden of HIV/AIDS, allied to the everyday struggles to find enough food, brought thoughts of suicide to her mind. 'But I knew that I needed to make my children's life a better experience than my own. By chance, a project taking place in my area made it possible for me to join a savings and credit co-operative, and begin my own small business. I used credit to begin animal fattening and petty trading and, within a year had taken back the land I had which I had rented out. I got seeds from the project, which was run by Self Help Africa, and began attending support meetings for people, and for the families of those who were living with HIV and AIDS. The awareness raising did a great deal to reduce the stigma and discrimination, as people began to learn more about HIV, and how it was transmitted'.

'I am working hard to make my children's life a better experience than my own. It is important that they get an education – especially the girls. I do not want them to inherit the problems from the previous generations. I want them to be emancipated from poverty, from HIV, and from subordination'.

Ayelech Mama's story is told with
the assistance of Munira Shemsudien

Munira Shemsudien is gender and HIV/AIDS Mainstreaming Programme Officer,
Self Help Africa, Ethiopia.

THREE VOICES

Hope is this child
Who makes a toy
From bits of wire
For tourists to buy

Inspiration's a Prince
Who brings us to a play,
Creating a spark
For another day.

Poverty's not always a lack
Of things like clothes upon your back.
A quenching of spirit is much more profound,
It keeps us chained right to the ground.

Jim Kirwan

*Jim Kirwan has been teaching English since 1973 in Coláiste Bhríde, Carnew
but also spent two years in the eighties in Lesotho, Southern Africa working in a High School.*

PEOPLE DON'T KNOW HOW LUCKY THEY ARE

People don't know how lucky they are,
With money, houses, streets and cars
And nothing to do
But give out about food, water, vaccines,
overcrowding in schools and the economic gloom.

Well there are people without food, water,
vaccines, shelter or even a school.

You don't know how lucky you are
That you have the power to give others a fresh start.

Emily Rose Byrne

*Emily Rose Byrne is a transition year student in Coláiste Bhríde Carnew
who captained the school's junior camogie team to championship victory in 2008.*

There was something almost heart-breaking about it. As I approached the clinic for the first time a child's toy was playing 'Happy Birthday' over and over. I had volunteered to help my friend Dr. Corrigan at her AIDS clinic in Dar es Salaam for one day a week. She was an Irish Medical Missionary sister and my task was to work with the children, all of them very young AIDS orphans. All had been born with AIDS and the clinic was trying new medicine to see if the situation could be reversed. For an adult the whole setup was very sad but the children mercifully did not see it that way. For me the saddest sight was of a very old grandmother. All she had left in world was her eight year old grandson and his twin brother and sister, barely one year old. Once a week these four trudged the dusty road to this clinic of hope. They came from afar, I was told, several bus journeys and a long walk. I watched them arrive and leave, one twin strapped to the back of the eight year old and the other strapped to the granny's back. They left sharing several plastic bags full of the week's food and medicine. They were a sorry sight but to me they were ever smiling, very gracious and so full of hope. I often wonder what happened to them.

Mary O'Hara

*Mary O'Hara is an Irish harpist and soprano singer who has risen
to the peak of success across the world but also spent twelve years
as a nun in Stanbrook Abbey after she was widowed at the age of 22.*

AID WORKER

I don't know where flies find food
Or how serum searches in a fallen vein.
I can't write about where you go.

I don't know how African light
Looks as it filters through dust
Raised by football on Sunday afternoons.

I don't know how rationed
Are medical supplies.
I can't tell which trees mark tribal lines.

I don't know what painkillers
Are proscribed or the difficulties
You'll find yourself in.

I can't prepare my mind.
I know I don't know, can't write or prepare
You so all I can offer is hope.

I know you go with your head held high.

Alan Garvey

Alan Garvey is a poet who believes in social justice.

A STOLEN SPIRIT

Their eyes are dead.
Their stares are numb,
As if a soul's been stolen.

They look at their hands,
At the growing filth
That has made an extra skin

These images pull at our heartstrings
But we just sigh and turn our heads
Back to our lives, forget about that mess.

Their heads tilt
An involuntary move
A tear falls down
And the spirit of life escapes
Never to return.

What have you done lately?

Rebecca Farry

Rebecca Farry is a transition year student in St. Peter's College, Dunboyne.

WORLD TO RIGHTS

Could you call the world to rights
If I told you the reward's nothing at all
Would you pipe down, just hold on tight
If the prize was just somebody else's life
The words don't come easy
When you don't practise what you preach
And all the goals we've set seem so, out of reach
You should know just what's at stake
And give thanks for every breath you take through your well fed mouth.

So don't avert your gaze, get sucked in
By appeals all over the television screen
Cos it's the only true-to-life broadcast you'll ever see.

Did you take in what they told you,
About a continent going to waste?
Does it just not suit you to change things,
Too inconvenient now you know your place?
Is someone else of no concern to you?
You've got other matters at hand,
what does it take to suck you in,
to make you understand?

Ben Cooper

Ben Cooper, a talented young singer/songwriter, is a transition year student in Coláiste Bhríde Carnew. This piece was written to music, which Ben performs on keyboard.

WHAT ABOUT THE REST?

I sat with my sister
Watching all their faces.
Young and old.
One hour,
One thousand and forty one lives.
Taken. Just from hunger.
Registered lives.
What about the rest?

Aaron Naylor

Aaron Naylor is a third class student at All Saints National School, Carnew, Co. Wicklow.

Acknowledgements

We would like to thank all those who sent in submissions
for this collaborative publication. Due to the huge
response, we were unable to include all submissions.
We would also like to extend our sincere appreciation to
all those who made this book happen.

Thank you for taking the time.

...

St. Peter's College Dunboyne in collaboration with
Coláiste Bhríde Carnew would like to thank Irish Aid
for its support and generous funding towards this
project, and would also like to thank Self Help Africa
and all the other NGOs for their advice and guidance.